I0762664

Little Mitchie

HOVER BiKES

Joanne Mattern

CREATING YOUNG NONFICTION READERS

Little Mitchie books spark curiosity and support early nonfiction reading for students in Grades 2-3. Designed to build vocabulary, support second language learners, and prepare readers for middle-grade content, each book includes helpful tips for parents and educators to build confidence and deepen understanding of the world.

TIPS FOR READING NONFICTION WITH BEGINNING READERS

Talk about Nonfiction

Begin by explaining that nonfiction books give us information that is true. The book will be organized around a specific topic or idea, and we may learn new facts through reading.

Look at the Parts

Most nonfiction books have helpful features. Our *Little Mitchie* titles include color photographs and graphic aids, a table of contents, a glossary, and an index. Share the purpose of these features with your reader.

Color Photos and Graphic Aids

A lot of information can be found by "reading" photos, charts, maps, and other graphic aids found within nonfiction texts. Help your reader learn more about the different ways information can be displayed.

Table of Contents

Located at the front of the book, this list shows the big ideas within the text and the page numbers where they can be found.

Glossary

Located at the back of the book, the glossary defines key words and phrases that are related to the topic. These words and phrases can be found in the text in colored type.

Index

Located at the back of the book, an index is an alphabetical list of topics and the page numbers where they can be found.

With a little help and guidance about reading nonfiction, you can feel good about introducing a young reader to the world of *Little Mitchie* nonfiction books.

Little Mitchie is an imprint of:

Mitchell Lane
PUBLISHERS

2001 SW 31st Avenue
Hallandale, FL 33009
mitchelllanepub.com

First Edition, 2027.

Author: Joanne Mattern
Designer: Bobbie Houser
Editor: Tricia Hoffman

Library of Congress Cataloging-in-Publication Data
Title: Hover Bikes / by Joanne Mattern

Description: Hallandale, FL :
Mitchell Lane Publishers, [2027]

Identifiers:
ISBN 979-8-89260-868-8 (library bound)
ISBN 979-8-89260-965-4 (eBook)

Library of Congress Control Number: 2026936187

PHOTO CREDITS
Alamy: Imaginechina Limited, 8; ZUMA Press, Inc., 12; MAXPPP, 15; Dreamstime: Keng62fa, 20; Public Domain: Volonaut, 11, 16, 17, 19; Wikipedia, 12; Shutterstock: haroldguevara, cover, 1; haroldguevara, 3, 4, 10, 18; tsuneomp, 5; Saku_rata160520, 6; 3DMI, 6, 22.

TABLE OF CONTENTS

Chapter One
TIME TO ZOOM! . . . 4

Chapter Two
HOVER BIKES ARE HERE . . . 10

Chapter Three
THE FUTURE OF HOVER BIKES . . . 18

LET'S LOOK AT A HOVER BIKE . . . 22
GLOSSARY . . . 23
FURTHER READING . . . 24
ON THE INTERNET . . . 24
INDEX . . . 24

Chapter One

TIME TO ZOOM!

Hailey and Uncle Mark were playing their favorite video game. A bike was flying through the air on-screen.

“I know you love the flying bikes in this video game,” Uncle Mark said. “How would you like to ride one for real?”

"Is that even possible?" Hailey asked.

"Someday it could be!" Uncle Mark said. He pulled up a video on his smartphone.

In the video, a strange **vehicle** sat on the grass. It looked like a motorcycle, but it had a **propeller** on each corner.

Hailey gasped as the bike rose into the sky. She couldn't believe what she was seeing!

"I can't wait to ride a **hover** bike!" she said.

WAY UP HIGH
A hover bike can fly about 16 feet (5 meters) in the air.

Chapter Two

HOVER BIKES ARE HERE

A hover bike is a vehicle that flies a short distance above the ground. It can reach speeds of nearly 125 miles (201 kilometers) per hour! Most hover bikes can only carry one rider at a time.

IN REAL LIFE

Hover bikes have been popular in books and movies for a long time. Now, these bikes are real!

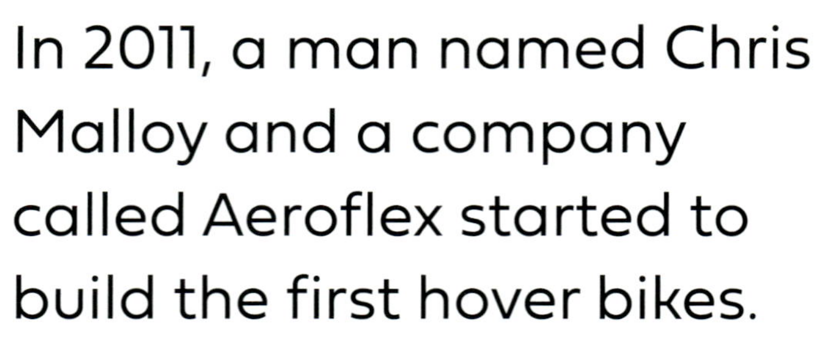

In 2011, a man named Chris Malloy and a company called Aeroflex started to build the first hover bikes.

At first, these bikes used **engines**, but that did not work so well. The inventors changed to propellers instead.

More than 10 years later, a Japanese company made a new hover bike called XTURISMO. This bike sits on two big **rotors**. Four smaller rotors are on the outside and work to keep the bike **stable**. The big rotors are powered by an engine, while the smaller ones run on batteries.

You can't ride the XTURISMO on the street. This bike only flies on a **test track** in Japan.

BIG PRICE TAG

The XTURISMO isn't cheap. It costs $500,000 or more!

A company called Volonaut showed off its Airbike in 2023. The Airbike is much smaller and lighter than the XTURISMO.

IT'S A SECRET!
The inventor of the Airbike will not explain how it flies.

Chapter Three

THE FUTURE OF HOVER BIKES

Hover bikes may be a lot of fun, but they are not ready to take over the skies just yet.

First, companies need to find a way to make the bikes safe—and affordable!

Someday, hover bikes could be used to fly over disasters. They could help find lost people, deliver supplies, or **patrol** dangerous places.

Maybe one day, you will own a hover bike!

LET'S LOOK AT A HOVER BIKE

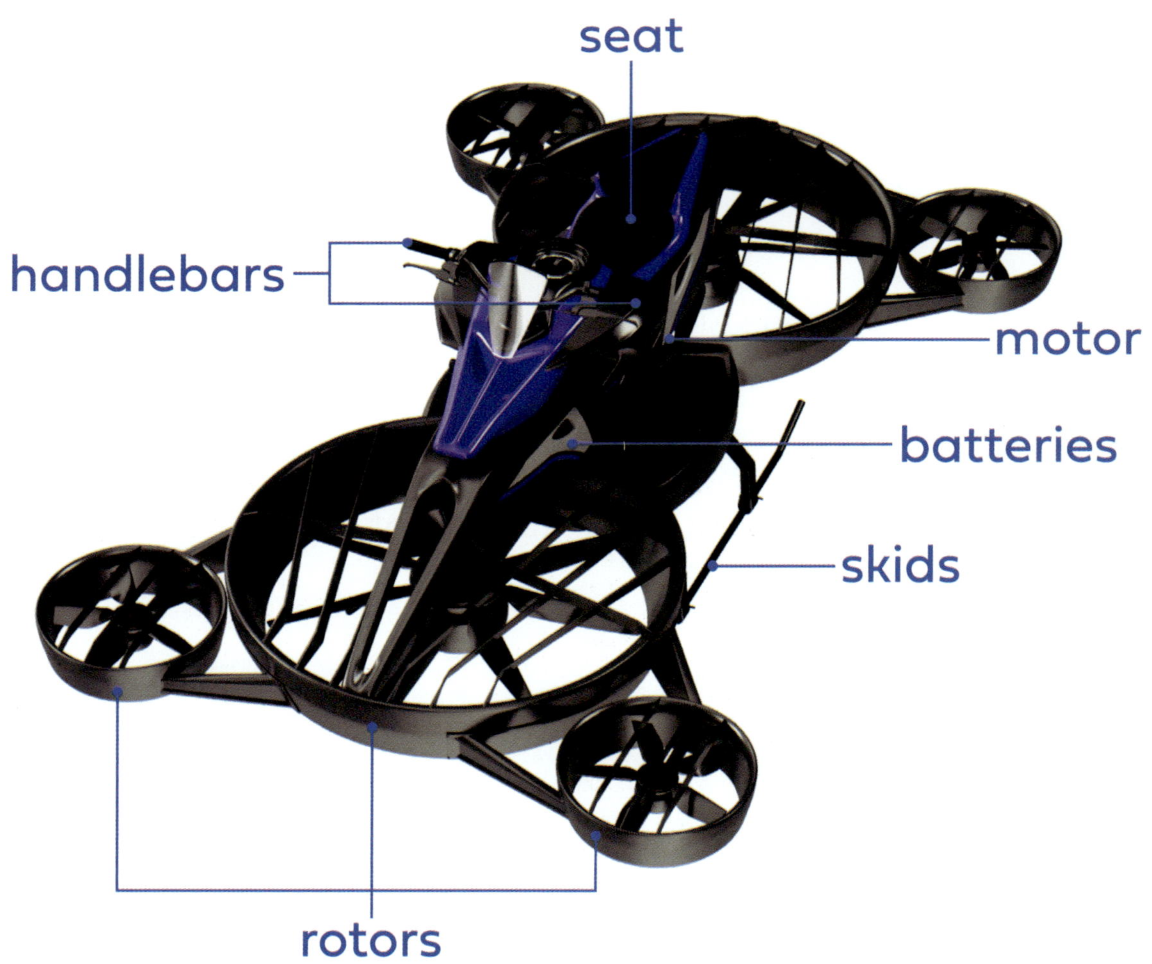

GLOSSARY

engines (en-jinz) machines that make something move by using gasoline, steam, or another energy source

hover (huhv-ur) to float in the air

patrol (puh-trohl) to travel around an area and make sure it is safe

propeller (pruh-pel-ur) a set of rotating blades that spin and provide force to push a vehicle forward

rotors (roh-turz) parts of a machine that spin

stable (stay-buhl) steady

test track (test trak) a designated area where new vehicles are tested

vehicle (vee-i-kuhl) a machine that carries people or goods from one place to another

FURTHER READING

Gagne, Tammy. *Cool Rides that Fly.* Capstone Press, 2020.

Hamilton, S.L. *Aerobatic Aircraft.* ABDO, 2022.

ON THE INTERNET

Motorcycle
https://kids.britannica.com/kids/article/motorcycle/400135
This Britannica Kids article describes the kind of bike that rides on the ground.

Star Wars or Real Life? Check Out This Hoverbike
www.cbc.ca/kidsnews/post/star-wars-or-real-life-check-out-this-hoverbike#
This CBC Kids News article describes what it is like to ride on a hover bike and also includes photos of bikes in action.

INDEX

Airbike 16, 17
battery 14, 22
cost 15
Malloy, Chris 12
rotors 14, 22
safety 19
Volonaut 16
XTURISMO 14, 15, 16